Insight Study Guide

Virginia Lee

The Great Gatsby

F. Scott Fitzgerald

insight

insight

F. Scott Fitzgerald's The Great Gatsby by Virginia Lee
Insight Study Guide series

Copyright © 2011 Insight Publications Pty Ltd

First published in 1997,
reprinted in 2006 by
Insight Publications Pty Ltd
ABN 57 005 102 983
89 Wellington Street
St Kilda VIC 3182
Australia
Tel: +61 3 9523 0044
Fax: +61 3 9523 2044
Email: books@insightpublications.com
Website: www.insightpublications.com

This edition published 2011 in the United States of America by
Insight Publications Pty Ltd, Australia.

ISBN-13: 978-1-875882-08-3

Library of Congress Control Number: 2011931352

Cover Design by The Modern Art Production Group
Cover Illustrations by The Modern Art Production Group,
istockphoto® and House Industries
Internal Design by Sarn Potter

Printed in the United States of America by Lightning Source
10 9 8 7 6 5 4 3 2 1

contents

CHARACTER MAP

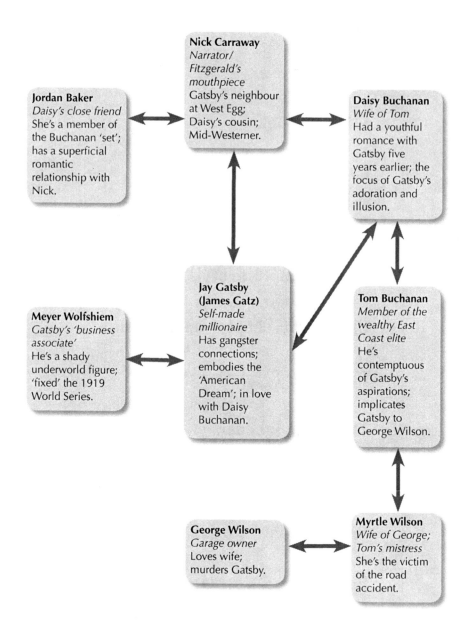

Nick Carraway
Narrator/ Fitzgerald's mouthpiece
Gatsby's neighbour at West Egg; Daisy's cousin; Mid-Westerner.

Jordan Baker
Daisy's close friend
She's a member of the Buchanan 'set'; has a superficial romantic relationship with Nick.

Daisy Buchanan
Wife of Tom
Had a youthful romance with Gatsby five years earlier; the focus of Gatsby's adoration and illusion.

Jay Gatsby (James Gatz)
Self-made millionaire
Has gangster connections; embodies the 'American Dream'; in love with Daisy Buchanan.

Meyer Wolfshiem
Gatsby's 'business associate'
He's a shady underworld figure; 'fixed' the 1919 World Series.

Tom Buchanan
Member of the wealthy East Coast elite
He's contemptuous of Gatsby's aspirations; implicates Gatsby to George Wilson.

George Wilson
Garage owner
Loves wife; murders Gatsby.

Myrtle Wilson
Wife of George; Tom's mistress
She's the victim of the road accident.

INTRODUCTION

F.Scott Fitzgerald was born in St Paul, Minnesota in 1896. He started writing at Princeton and had his first novel *This Side of Paradise* published in 1920. Four other novels followed: *The Beautiful and the Dammed* (1922), *The Great Gatsby* (1925), *Tender is the Night* (1934), and his final unfinished work, *The Last Tycoon* (published posthumously). He also wrote five volumes of short stories, including *The Crack-Up*, a selection of autobiographical pieces.

The relationship between Scott Fitzgerald's writing and his personal life has been well-documented. Readers of *The Great Gatsby* will recognise a correlation between Fitzgerald's Mid-Western background, the uncertain courtship of his wife, Zelda, the life they subsequently led together, and circumstances confronting some of the characters in the novel.

When Scott and Zelda did marry, after the success of *This Side of Paradise*, their lifestyle, first in New York and later in Europe, exemplified the extravagant, party-going hedonism of the Twenties.

Few writers have so successfully captured the spirit of their generation. Fitzgerald was both a perceptive, at times acerbic, commentator of his age and one of its most spectacular victims.

The self-destructive spiral of debt and alcoholism which compromised the Fitzgeralds' life together brought about heart ache, physical decline and finally, premature death at the age of forty-four.

CONTEXT & BACKGROUND

The context

The Great Gatsby is set in America in the 'Jazz Age', a period of great hedonism that reflects people's determination to forget the suffering and losses of the First World War. In America this was also a period of great economic expansion which gave people unprecedented wealth; it was also a period of "moral confusion" as the novel shows.

The Great Gatsby is set in the summer of 1922, at the height of what Fitzgerald himself christened 'the Jazz Age'. It is important to have some understanding of the context in which the novel is set.

The decade between the First World War and the Great Depression was a volatile, ebullient period when society was bent on recovery, psychological as well as economic. The defining influence of the era was the Great War. Its carnage and trauma – ten million dead and approximately twenty million wounded – was unprecedented. (Interestingly, Nick Carraway seems to have 'enjoyed' a very sheltered war, as did Fitzgerald himself. If you wish to learn more about the appalling reality of life in the trenches, *Good-bye to all That* by Robert Graves or, more recently, *Birdsong* by Sebastian Faulks will give you some idea.) Post-war America saw a population shift to the cities, the emergence of modern industry, high wages and lavish spending. There was a frenetic determination to forget the war and make the most of the moment. Jazz, sensual, subversive and indigenously American, was the popular music of the day. Emancipated women enjoyed a new independence.

Disillusionment and moral confusion

However, the mood of superficial optimism masked a pervasive sense of disillusionment and moral confusion. In 1922, T.S. Elliot published *The Waste Land*; its pessimistic vision seemed to encapsulate the notion that humanity had lost its way. Consumerism was proving an inadequate substitute for the old moral certainties. Daisy Buchanan's plaintive cry, 'What'll we do with ourselves this afternoon... and the day after that, and the next thirty years?' (p.113) expresses the restlessness and spiritual impoverishment of the 'lost generation'. Fitzgerald in *The Great Gatsby* brilliantly and succinctly explores the tensions and contradictions of the period. On the one hand, we are presented with the glamour and exhilaration which has become synonymous with the Twenties; on the other, we see the despair and dislocation which lie just beneath the surface.

Prohibition

Key Point

Prohibition is the key factor to our understanding of Gatsby's fabulous wealth but disclosure of this is indirect, part of the puzzle Nick and the reader have to solve about Gatsby's existence.

Traditional values and mores were flouted in this period which was also the Prohibition era. Spearheaded by the Temperance movement, Prohibition was introduced in the United States in 1920. For the next three years, until 1923, the manufacture, transportation, sale and possession of alcohol was forbidden. Ultimately, the impracticality of legislating on a question of public morality was acknowledged and the law was repealed as unworkable. In the meantime, a black market flourished, as 'bootleggers' orchestrated the illicit production and sale of liquor. (See also note 19, p.175 in the novel.) Corruption was rife. Because the legislation was never adequately enforced by the authorities, Prohibition, in fact, encouraged contempt for the law which was flagrantly disregarded by almost everyone.

In the novel we gradually realise Gatsby's connections with bootlegging. Some important clues are his 'gonnegtions' with Wolfshiem (pp. 68-69), the calls from Chicago (p.49), Gatsby's shiftiness with Nick about his line of business (p.87)), Tom Buchanan's direct accusations (p.127) and his lonely funeral. Tom Buchanan's contempt for Gatsby is based on this and underpins his recognition that Gatsby can make no claims to a respectable social standing whatever, although Fitzgerald ironically shows that Tom is morally bankrupt himself in other ways. Gatsby's involvement in bootlegging exposes the corrupt side of Gatsby's character which has to be reconciled with his "pure" love for Daisy, something Nick the narrator admires and elevates. As the reader you need to weigh these factors in your summing up of Gatsby.

The broader significance of the Prohibition is its importance in revealing the contradictory values of the times and the new emphasis on the "get-rich-quick" mentality pervading the American culture.

GENRE, STRUCTURE, STYLE & LANGUAGE

GENRE

KEY POINT

The Great Gatsby is a novel of considerable beauty and simplicity yet intricacy. Its distinguishing features are Fitzgerald's poetic prose, the fragmented but absorbing story, the use of the laconic first-person narrator, the creation of the elusive character of Gatsby and his fated love for Daisy, and the subtle depiction of inter-related social and moral issues in the American society of the period.

In 1922, Fitzgerald wrote a letter to his editor, Maxwell Perkins, expressing his intentions for his new novel. It would be:

'Something new...beautiful and simple, and intricately patterned'

The Great Gatsby is all that. It is a complex, multi-layered text which is rewarded by close reading. The novel is simultaneously a poignant love story, an exploration of the 'American Dream', a superb evocation of American society in the Twenties, and a biting social satire.

The story

KEY POINT

This novel tells a story of fatal obsession and as such could fall prey to the formula writing of popular novels. However, Fitzgerald creates a deeply moving account of Gatsby's quest for emotional fulfillment, enriched by the exploration of the moral problems of elevating the acquisition of wealth above all else.

The Great Gatsby is firstly the story of a fatal obsession. Jay Gatsby's determination to succeed in a world which is defined by materialism, and win back the heart of the woman he adores provides the bones of the novel. For nearly five years, Gatsby has been sustained by loyalty, optimism, energy and single-minded passion. The illusion that Daisy Buchanan will reciprocate this commitment is one of the sad fallacies on which his dream is based. Despite her charm and vulnerability, Daisy is essentially a shallow woman who is too dependent on her husband to leave him. When she and Gatsby are briefly reunited, the impossibility of recapturing the intensity of their past relationship becomes self-evident.

Notwithstanding this, Gatsby's dream of romantic fulfillment moves beyond Daisy herself to become a heroic defiance of reality. Daisy's limitations, the barriers imposed by her marriage – even the possibility that the past was not exactly as he remembers it – none of these truths are allowed to impinge on the vision of the future he tries to create with her. The realisation, when it comes, that he has been deluded brings about a spiritual death, which prefigures his literal death.

Fitzgerald explores the difficulty of individuals maintaining moral integrity in a material society which values the acquisition of wealth above all else. Gatsby's quest for emotional fulfillment becomes inextricably bound up with his material ambitions. Having dreamt as a boy of embracing a destiny which leaves behind the poverty and mediocrity of his background, he then meets Daisy. Their love affair provides a focus for his ambition, running in tandem with it. He says to Nick '...What was the use of doing great things if I could have a better time telling her what I was going to do?' (p.143). However Daisy is very rich and he is still poor. After she throws him over to marry Tom Buchanan, Gatsby's despair is such that he is especially vulnerable to the insidious influence of Meyer Wolfshiem and his 'gonnegtions'. Gatsby yields to their corrupt ethos, having decided that the end *will* justify the means. Some premonition of the elusive and precarious foundation on which his dream is based visits him when he returns to Louisville:

> He stretched out his hand desperately as if to snatch only a wisp
> of air, to save a fragment of the spot that she had made lovely for
> him. But it was all going by too fast now for his blurred eyes and he
> knew that he had lost that part of it, the freshest and the best, forever
> (pp.145-46).

Four key locations

This fraught story of love and hope is set against a rich tapestry of images which collectively evoke various aspects of American society. Nick's Mid-Western background identifies him with the traditional values which are coming under threat from social upheaval and the prevailing climate of self-indulgence. Arriving East, he is actually confronted with a kaleidoscope of conflicting images which reflect the confused and paradoxical nature of the period. Four key locations present themselves. The wealth and ephemeral glamour of the East is exemplified by New York which acts as a magnet to those, like Nick, who hope to exploit its opportunities and challenges. At first Nick finds the city beautiful and exciting; its unique skyline rising up 'in white heaps and sugar lumps all built with a wish out of nonolfactory money' (p.67). East Egg is the home of the establishment; its wealth and power are inherited, its traditions entrenched. West Egg, by contrast, attracts the 'nouveau riche'. Their 'in-your-face' spending power smacks of vulgarity and pretension, and a careless disregard for the constraints of the past. Mid-way between New York and West Egg is the 'valley of ashes', a desolate wasteland where live the 'ash-grey men' (p.26). This is the stark underbelly of a society which has replaced faith with consumerism.

First-person narration and Nick Carraway

KEY POINT

The first-person narration in this novel is highly distinctive. Nick Carraway acts as a filter through whom ideas and characters are reflected and mediated. His limited viewpoint is broadened through accounts of other witnesses to key events and his observations on characters and social and moral and issues are subtle and ironic. Through him Fitzgerald is able to critique the period under scrutiny.

Nick Carraway unfolds Gatsby's story in the first person. The ways in which Fitzgerald has used the first-person narration is one of the strengths of the novel for Nick is created as a character in his own right who also reflects on the other characters and issues of the story he tells. He is influential in shaping the way we read the story and our responses to key events. At the very beginning of the novel we learn that Nick is back home in the mid-West of America, reflecting on his time in New York. He wants moral certainty, something his experiences in the East have denied him.

Fitzgerald highlights the moral contradictions through Nick's increasingly critical eyes. Equally, the individuals with whom he comes into contact come under scrutiny. By the end of the novel, after Gatsby's death, the East has been stripped of its attraction for him; rather, it is 'haunted ...distorted beyond (his) eyes' power of correction' (p.167).

Nick's disillusionment is profound; he wants 'no more riotous excursions with privileged glimpses into the human heart' (p.8). Only Gatsby is exempt from this reaction. Nick comes to value Gatsby's 'extraordinary gift for hope', the 'romantic readiness' (p.8) which sets him apart from everyone else. And herein lies the paradox at the heart of Gatsby's persona. While he has succumbed to the corrupting power of wealth in order to facilitate his ambition, he retains a purity of heart and purpose which transcends that corruption:

> Gatsby believed in the green light, the orgastic future that year
> by year recedes before us. It eluded us then, but that's no matter
> – tomorrow we will run faster, stretch out our arms further... (p.172).

Nick and Gatsby as registers of the moral temper of the age

Nick senses that Gatsby's 'incorruptible dream' represents a vital touchstone, a spiritual initiative, which a secular age either gets wrong or runs the risk of losing altogether. We are indeed 'boats against the current' (p.172). The green light at the end of the Buchanans' dock, across the Sound from Gatsby's empty showpiece of a house, comes to symbolise the desire and romantic yearning which is an integral component of our humanity. At the same time, hope can too easily become perverted into greed. Gatsby's predicament underscores an archetypal modern dilemma and thus has a tragic resonance. He is a victim of the 'foul dust' which floats 'in the wake of his dreams' (p.8). In an uncaring society governed by the capitalist ethos, it preys on us all.

STRUCTURE

KeY POiNt

The novel's structure, the order in which events and information are revealed to the reader, is complex. The novel does not develop chronologically which means the reader has to fit the pieces of the jigsaw together and use later information to modify earlier interpretations. Fitzgerald's use of the narrator Nick Carraway makes this process seem natural and creates tension and suspense for the reader.

The structure of *The Great Gatsby* is a complex one. Nick Carraway tells the story in retrospect, approximately one year after the main events of the summer of 1922. Nick's role in the novel, as both the narrator *and* a character in his own right, gives the narrative its particular flavour and focus. Nick reports events as he witnesses them and communicates the facts of Gatsby's and Daisy' relationship in the order in which he learns them. This means, from the reader's perspective, the chronology is scrambled. The truth of Gatsby's character and history emerge gradually. Information is apportioned out piece by piece, determined by Nick's circumstances, and filtered through his perceptions. For the times when Nick is not present, he reconstructs events for the reader, by paraphrasing the reminiscences of other characters – Gatsby, Jordan, Meyer Wolfshiem. In positioning Nick well beyond the point of crisis, Fitzgerald is able to maintain an equilibrium between his immediate impression of various happenings and his subsequent overview of the period in question.

STYLE AND LANGUAGE

Key Point

This novel combines realism – making events and characters seem life-like or credible – with a range of poetic symbols which gather meaning and significance as the novel progresses. These, together with the intricate patterning referred to earlier, create layers of meaning which resonate throughout the novel.

The language of the novel is both economical and poetic, effectively combining social realism and metaphor. On the one hand, we have Nick Carraway's narration, the tone of which is crisp, reflective, ironic. He observes and appraises the behaviour of his fellow New Yorkers in an incisive, often comic voice. By contrast, on occasions the language becomes so rich in imagery that it creates an impressionistic world; a sense of dream-like enchantment, or nightmare.

Fitzgerald employs the method of selecting details and investing these with significant, often symbolic meaning. Recurring images – cars, clocks, ghosts, death, moonlight, eyes – invite the reader to focus on a symbolic landscape which highlights Fitzgerald's thematic concerns. On close examination, we see that apparently disparate elements contribute to an integrated whole. The chapter-by-chapter analysis which follows will give you some understanding and appreciation of the intricate 'patterning' of Fitzgerald's work.

CHAPTER-BY-CHAPTER ANAYLSIS

Chapter I

The novel is narrated by Nick Carraway, an affluent young man from a prominent Mid-Western family. He has been educated at New Haven and seen active service during the Great War, an experience which leaves him restless and dissatisfied.

Accordingly, he decides to go East to learn the bond business, taking with him his father's advice to reserve judgement and remember that not everyone has enjoyed the same advantages as the Carraways. He leases a house on the tip of the promontory known as West Egg, twenty miles from the city of New York, next door to an ostentatious mansion owned by a Mr. Gatsby and opposite the glittering residences of fashionable East Egg.

One warm summer's evening, Nick drives over to visit the Buchanan's. Tom Buchanan is an old friend from college; an arrogant, egocentric individual with a powerful physical presence and a bullying manner. Daisy, his wife, is Nick's second cousin. Beautiful, vulnerable, she draws men to her effortlessly. The charm of her voice, 'low and thrilling,' evokes promise and intrigue, and contains an excitement 'that men who had cared for her found difficult to forget' (p.14). The other guest present is a school friend of Daisy's from Louisville, a successful young golf champion named Jordan Baker. Before dinner, Nick's neighbour Gatsby is casually mentioned and Daisy reacts sharply.

Conversation during dinner is monopolised by Tom and his discussion of a book which he has just read and been impressed by. When he is called to the telephone, Daisy excuses herself and also leaves the room. In their absence, Jordan explains to Nick that Tom has a mistress in New York – apparently the relationship is common knowledge. By the time the Buchanans return, the atmosphere is strained.

Nick and Daisy talk privately on the porch after dinner and when Nick asks about her little daughter, Daisy confesses her unhappiness and cynicism. Tom's infidelity has been a feature of their marriage for years. They move back inside and Daisy announces her intention of encouraging the relationship between Nick and Jordan. Irritably, Tom criticises Jordan's independence. As Nick is leaving, the Buchanans ask him about his rumoured engagement back West, a circumstance he denies (p.24).

Altogether, Nick feels discomforted by the evening. Upon his return to West Egg, he observes his neighbour, Mr Gatsby, alone in the adjoining garden. Nick represses his first instinct to make contact as it becomes evident that Gatsby values his solitude. His concentration is focused out towards the bay, on a green light which shines at the end of the dock opposite.

How Nick, the first-person narrator, influences the reader

Writing in the first person, Nick's perspective invites the reader's complicity. He presents himself as a tolerant young man, a sympathetic listener, someone whose judgement may be relied on. Hence we understand his point of view to be the true and impartial one. His conclusions with regard to the characters, their relationships with each other, and the way in which events unfold, will have authority, a sort of moral currency. At the same time, is there an unconscious irony in his observation that 'the intimate revelations of young men ….are usually plagiaristic and marred by obvious suppressions' (p.7). Will Nick's story also be marred obvious suppressions? Is Fitzgerald warning readers to evaluate Nick's perspective just as carefully as that of the other characters?

Nick and Gatsby – the first link

There is also an early connection established between Nick and Gatsby. Reserving judgements is a 'matter of infinite hope.' Equally, Gatsby has an 'extraordinary gift for hope.' Nick clearly admires this capacity and the 'romantic readiness…never found in any other person'(p. 8). What, then, are we to make of Nick's evaluation of the man whom the title calls 'great'?

> Gatsby turned out alright at the end; it is what preyed on Gatsby, what foul dust floated in the wake of his dreams that temporarily closed out my interest in the abortive sorrows and shortwinded elations of men (p. 8).

One of your tasks in studying the novel will be to determine what this summation ultimately reveals about both Gatsby *and* Nick.

The Mid-West and the East

'Instead of being the warm centre of the world, the Middle West now seemed like the ragged edge of the universe' (p.9). Nick's exodus east is mirrored by other characters in the book: the Buchanans, for example, have also come from the Mid-West, as has Gatsby himself. In this chapter, we have an immediate contrast set up between the West – dull, parochial, and the East, glamorous, sophisticated, full of promise and opportunity. During the Buchanans' dinner, Nick observes with appreciation the differences between the ambiance and conversation of the evening, and a similar one in the West. Nevertheless, despite the surface attractions of New York and its society, the values promoted by those who live there will prove disillusioning. Nick's growing awareness of the corruption which underpins the glamour and the energy, and his yearning to return to the more innocent values of his past is one of the key issues in the text.

Tom and Daisy Buchanan

The Buchanans exemplify this tension. While Nick's relationship with them is of long-standing, it is essentially superficial. On the face of it, their lifestyle is to be envied; defined as it is by privilege and enormous wealth. Nick acknowledges the beauty and elegance that money can create. Tom and Daisy's home, with its glorious garden, french windows, gracefully draped, and 'bright, rosy-coloured' spaces, is testimony to its seductive power (p.12). The Buchanans' money is 'old' money with its connotations of breeding and taste and solidarity. By contrast, Gatsby is one of the 'new' rich. His mansion, a grand but garish copy of a French hotel, simply demonstrates what money can *not* buy. At the same time, the Buchanans are drifters, literally and spiritually. Their lifestyle is dictated by whim; they travel restlessly 'wherever people played polo and were rich together' (p.12). It is a sterile, empty existence, devoid of real values, and it affords neither one true satisfaction. The marriage is not happy. Money is not a substitute for a sense of purpose or successful relationships. Nevertheless, despite Daisy's protestations of unhappiness, she remains with Tom, with no apparent intention of leaving him and no awareness that she is compromising herself by doing so. Further, Nick receives the uncomfortable impression that her loyalties to her husband run deeper than she is prepared to admit, and that her shared confidences amount to a performance for his, Nick's, benefit. This 'membership in a rather distinguished secret society to which she and Tom belonged' (p.22) has tragic consequences for Gatsby later on.

Nick's first glimpse of Gatsby

Nick' first sighting of his elusive neighbour at the end of Chapter I is also significant. Initially struck by Gatsby's proprietorial manner, Nick senses his separateness and isolation, and an internal tension which seems to have as its focus the green light over the bay. We subsequently discover that this is the light at the end of Tom and Daisy's dock. Nick watches him stretch out his arms towards it and, though he does not understand the significance of the gesture, he recognizes its unresolved poignancy. We are left with a sense of mystery.

Chapter II

Between West Egg and New York is a grey wasteland, the 'valley of ashes' (p.26). Presiding over this dreary landscape is a huge billboard advertising the practice of Dr. T. J. Eckleburg, an oculist. Tom Buchanan's mistress, Myrtle Wilson, lives 'on the edge of the waste land' (p.27) with her husband George, who runs the local garage. One Sunday, Nick accompanies Tom up to New York when Tom insists on stopping there to see her.

George Wilson is an unprepossessing individual who has absorbed the defeated air of his surroundings. He and Tom exchange some perfunctory remarks about a car which Tom is selling, when his wife enters. Though she is no beauty, 'in the middle thirties and faintly stout' (p.28), she exudes a sensuous energy that is both challenging and provocative. After making an excuse to her husband, Myrtle arranges to meet Tom and Nick, and they journey up to New York together. At the station, Myrtle makes a number of purchases, including a puppy. They drive to an apartment near Central Park which Tom has provided for his mistress (p.31), and despite his reluctance, Nick finds himself joining them for a drink.

What follows is a drunken, increasingly hazy afternoon. A number of people arrive: the McKees, a photographer and his wife, neighbours from the downstairs flat, and Myrtle's sister, Catherine. While Myrtle swans around the apartment, playing the grand lady, her guests make desultory conversation and drink whisky. Nick discovers that Catherine has been to one of Gatsby's parties and she repeats the rumour that he is a wealthy relation of the Kaiser's. She also tells him that Daisy won't divorce Tom because she is a Catholic – an excuse Nick knows to be a lie. Myrtle stridently informs the company what a mistake her marriage was and later, more confidentially to Nick, describes her first meeting with Tom.

At some point, late in the evening, by which stage everyone is very drunk, an argument breaks out between Tom and Myrtle as to whether Myrtle has the right to mention Daisy's name. In a sudden, shocking response, Tom breaks his mistress's nose. The superficial goodwill immediately dissolves in confusion and panic. Nick accompanies McKee downstairs, and after briefly looking at the latter's portfolio, finds his way home alone.

The waste land – the 'valley of ashes'

The desolate landscape between West Egg and New York must surely be one of the most joyless in literature. It is a no-man's land – reminiscent of the no man's land between the trenches intersecting the battlefields of the First World War, from which the Allies and their German foes devastated both each other and the once-lush French country-side. (See also note 9, p.174). The 'valley of ashes' is a parody of fertile farming land, where 'ashes grow like wheat into ridges and hills and grotesque gardens' (p.27). Bordered by 'a small foul river', even the road shrinks away from contact with it. Grey dust covers the dwellings and the people who live there. Their lives are empty; they merely go through the motions. George Wilson is one such individual, a defeated man who has neither the respect of his wife nor his colleagues. Interestingly, the 'white ashen dust' which veils his suit and his hair (p.28), as it veils everything else in the vicinity, does not touch his wife. Is this because her sheer contempt for her environment wills it away?

The giant eyes of Dr. Eckleburg, all-seeing and all-knowing, are an equally powerful metaphor. In a godless landscape, where materialism and the pursuit of self-gratification have replaced more substantial values, an advertising billboard acts as the ironic overseer of the exploits of the individuals who pass by. The mocking anonymity of the eyes – for 'they look out of no face' (p.26) – reinforces their true indifference.

The party at Myrtle's apartment

This is a very important episode as it reveals the characters of Nick, Myrtle and in particular Tom Buchanan, as well as signifying the spiritual emptiness of people's lives.

The increasingly surrealistic gathering at Myrtle Wilson's apartment, in which Nick finds himself an unwilling participant, is particularly revealing, both in terms of the characters themselves and the barrenness of their lives. The lack of taste with which the flat is furnished (p.31) presents an uncomfortable contrast to the effortless elegance of the Buchanan interiors. Having changed her clothes several times, Myrtle plays hostess with an affectation and self-consciousness that merely serves to expose her pretensions for the rather pathetic delusions that they are. Tom clearly does not love her. While the immediate physical gratification which follows their first meeting suggests a mutual ruthlessness, it is he, by virtue of his money and power, who has the upper hand in the relationship. He is deceiving her with regard to the true state of his marriage and has constructed an elaborate fiction to justify the fact that he remains with Daisy. The crude violence which he demonstrates towards Myrtle at the end of the evening highlights the contempt in which he truly holds her. She is a necessary convenience, no more nor less. His action also demonstrates the arrogance and aggression which is so much a part of his psyche.

Emerging themes and Nick's increasingly ambivalent attitude

It is no accident that this scene is viewed through an alcoholic haze, with its accompanying distortions. In these first two chapters, Fitzgerald is effectively building up a picture of a collection of individuals whose lives lack commitment to anything except the moment. Faith, spirituality, hope, love – these are qualities notably absent in their dealings with each other. The defining yardstick of success is money: hence in the eyes of Myrtle and her friends, George is a failure, while Tom and his kind are to be admired. The world is divided into winners and losers. The veracity (accuracy) of this premise is one of the questions raised by the text. Even at this early stage, Nick's ambivalence is evident. He is both a part of the scene, contributing to it, and at the same time, aloof from it; preserving a detachment which is not quite judgemental, but certainly contains an element of scrutiny. 'I was within and without, simultaneously enchanted and repelled by the inexhaustible variety of life' (p. 37).

Chapter III

Nick's next-door neighbour, Gatsby, holds large, lavishly-catered parties which have become legendary among rich, well-connected New Yorkers. The first evening that Nick goes over, he believes he is one of the few who has actually been invited. Upon arriving, he makes an abortive attempt to find his host and then, to his relief, meets up with Jordan Baker. He joins her party and they spend most of the night together. Among the guests, there is considerable speculation as to Gatsby's antecedents. Some say he was a German spy during the War; others repeat the rumour that he killed a man.

Nick and Jordan share supper with the group she came with, then leave them, ostensibly to find Gatsby. They do not have immediate success, but gradually Nick starts to enjoy himself, as the tempo of the party escalates. Sometime after midnight, Nick and Jordan find themselves seated at a table with a young man who has served in the same division as Nick during the War. After talking together for a while, Nick discovers that this is Gatsby. His first impression of his host is favourable; Gatsby's smile contains a wonderful quality of understanding; it is a smile that seems to reassure and affirm, and Nick falls under its spell. At the same time, he also senses that Gatsby is presenting a facade. His curiosity is aroused. He observes Gatsby's aloofness from the crowd and the fact that, unlike his guests, he is not drinking.

Gatsby then requests to speak to Jordan alone and, bemused, she accompanies him into the house. The party starts to break up; most of the guests are, by now, maudlin and argumentative. Nick is about to leave, when Jordan returns and explains that Gatsby has told her an amazing story. She asks Nick to call her. On his way out, Nick witnesses a bizarre scene. Someone's car has landed in the ditch beside the road outside Gatsby's mansion: a wheel has come off but both occupants of the vehicle, who are considerably under the weather, disclaim responsibility.

Nick tells the reader a little of his life in New York. Work occupies most of his attention, but, despite the occasional feeling of loneliness, he begins to enjoy the 'racy, adventurous feel' (p.57) of the city. He resumes contact with Jordan Baker and becomes close to her. The recognition that she is 'incurably dishonest' (p.58) is not an impediment to the relationship, although her careless driving provokes Nick's censure.

Gatsby's parties

The scale on which Gatsby entertains is, by any standards, extraordinary. Nick watches, intrigued, as guests come and go throughout the summer. 'In his blue gardens men and girls came and went like moths among the whisperings and the champagne and the stars' (p.41). His parties exemplify the carefree, hedonistic mood of the Jazz Age. Alcohol flows freely (despite Prohibition – see p. 3), emancipated young women drift from partner to partner; there is a frenzied determination to have a good time at whatever cost. In a time of lavish spending and high living, Gatsby's 'greatness' is assured.

However, the meticulous catering on the one hand, and the careless indifference as to who actually attends his parties, on the other, suggests a contradiction. He is obviously wealthy and presumably generous, but seems to derive no personal satisfaction from the occasions. He does not even know most of his guests. In turn, they are simply necessary props, along with the food, the lighting, the orchestration. What is Gatsby's purpose? Who is he trying to impress? We find ourselves asking the same questions as other characters in the book. The mystery surrounding him gives rise to all sorts of exaggerated stories. As Nick observes 'young men didn't ...drift coolly out of nowhere and buy a palace on Long Island Sound' (p.50).

Gatsby's persona has been painstakingly constructed – even the books in his bookcase are real. Nevertheless, even as Nick succumbs to Gatsby's charm, he is alert to a self-consciousness which threatens to undermine the image ... '(his) elaborate formality of speech just missed being absurd... I'd got a strong impression that he was picking his words with care (p. 49). Nick also recognizes Gatsby's essential detachment from the frenetic gaiety which surrounds him. At its height, he stands alone on his marble steps, 'looking from one group to another with approving eyes' (p. 51). He is like the director on a movie set; the scene being played out before him meets with his expectations, but he is not a part of it. Again, Nick's final image of his host is one of isolation, as he stands in front of his now-abandoned mansion. We are reminded of our first sighting of him at the end of Chapter I – there is the same sense of yearning and lack of fulfillment.

The car motif

KEY POINT

A motif is a recurring image. The car, a symbol of the new mobility and freedom of the period, is also linked with violence through bodily harm as well with the themes of irresponsibility and carelessness.

The car motif is a recurring one throughout the novel and the car accident at the end of Gatsby's party, farcical though it is, is the precursor of several such accidents. Jordan is also, by her own admission, a careless driver, but prefers to throw the onus of responsibility onto others, rather than accept it herself. This idea of individuals assuming liability for their actions emerges as a key concern of Fitzgerald's. It will become evident that the careless abrogation of responsibility can have destructive consequences.

Chapter IV

Nick chronicles some of the people who enjoy Gatsby's hospitality in the summer of 1922. The list is long and includes representatives from East and West Egg society, theatrical types, famous and infamous names.

One afternoon, Nick has lunch with Gatsby in New York. As they drive up to town in Gatsby's 'gorgeous' car, Gatsby divulges a little of his background. He tells Nick that he inherited his fortune from wealthy parents, was educated at Oxford University, subsequently travelled throughout Europe, and served with distinction during the War – all the time trying to forget 'something very sad that had happened to [him]

(p. 64). Just when Nick decides it is all nonsense, Gatsby shows him a couple of souvenirs that seem genuine. He has a request to make of Nick. However, rather than explain himself, he has asked Jordan, with whom Nick is having tea, to act as his intermediary. As they near the city, Gatsby is pulled over for speeding. He shows the policeman a Christmas card from the Commissioner of Police and is waved on. (p.67)

They have lunch with Meyer Wolfshiem, a gambler and business associate of Gatsby's, with criminal connections. After he leaves them, Gatsby confides to Nick that Wolfshiem is the man who 'fixed' the World Series of 1919. (p. 71) As Nick is settling the bill, he catches sight of Tom Buchanan. He introduces Gatsby to Tom and notes his discomfort at the meeting. Indeed, Gatsby disappears immediately afterwards.

Subsequently, from Jordan, Nick learns of the love affair between Gatsby and Daisy. They had met five years earlier, when Gatsby was a young lieutenant and Daisy the belle of Louisville. To Jordan, who was two years younger, the undisguised adoration with which Gatsby looked at Daisy left an indelible impression. When he was posted overseas, the romance was put under pressure. By the following season, Daisy was 'gay again' (p. 73), and a little while after that, she married Tom Buchanan 'with more pomp and circumstance than Louisville ever knew before' (p. 74). Only Jordan knew that the day before, she had gotten very drunk after receiving a letter, presumably from Gatsby, and had threatened to call the whole event off. Surprisingly, the Buchanan marriage seemed a happy one at first, until Tom's philandering became blatant. Daisy lost all contact with Gatsby. Until it was mentioned by Nick some weeks before, she had not heard his name in years.

Gatsby's request is as follows: he wants Nick to invite Daisy to tea so he can 'come over' some afternoon. Jordan explains to Nick that he particularly wants her to see his house. The chapter concludes with Nick kissing Jordan.

Significance of the list of Gatsby's party-goers.

What is Fitzgerald's purpose in commencing this chapter with the long, chaotic list of individuals who come to Gatsby's house throughout the summer? Clearly he wants to leave the reader with a sense of the season's relentless partying, in which one day runs into the next, and the guests conduct themselves 'according to the rules of behaviour associated with an amusement park' (p. 43). The bizarre names of the party-goers – the Fishguards, the Ripley Snells, the Catlips, and so on, and their even more bizarre behaviour – one guest runs over another's hand – conveys a surreal mood of collective mayhem. There is a satirical edge to Nick's comment that most who accept Gatsby's hospitality 'paid him the subtle tribute of knowing nothing whatever about him' (p. 60)

The romantic relationship between Gatsby and Daisy

At this point, the shadowy figure of Gatsby starts to come into sharper focus. We learn of the past romantic relationship between Gatsby and Daisy. We discover Gatsby's purpose in buying the house on the other side of the bay from Daisy and constructing a lifestyle, the rotations of which will eventually draw her into his orbit. When Nick hears their story for the first time, Gatsby 'came alive'; he was 'delivered suddenly from the womb of his purposeless splendour' (p. 76). Nick is impressed both by the force of his commitment and the patient, diffident way in which he goes about achieving his objective. He has waited five years and bought a mansion where he 'dispensed starlight to casual moths' (p. 76) in order to resume modest contact with her. We have our first intimation of an obsession that is all-encompassing.

At the same time, Jordan's narrative raises certain questions with regard to Daisy's position. Why did she marry Tom Buchanan, when she obviously retained strong feelings for Gatsby? Jordan tells Nick that when the Buchanan's returned from their honeymoon, she'd 'never seen a girl so mad about her husband' (p. 75). What does this mercurial turnaround tell us about Daisy?

Gatsby's 'real' life

We also learn something of Gatsby's 'real' life. Yet another rumour prefaces the chapter, the possibility that he is a bootlegger. (Remember, the novel is set during the Prohibition era – a time when organised crime flourished). Gatsby's association with Meyer Wolfshiem – a man who should be in jail – hints at a shady underworld of criminal connections.

Moreover, we are left wondering about the 'favour' that Gatsby performed for the Commissioner of Police, a service which now gives him exemption from the law.

New York

Note Nick and Gatsby's entry into New York. Sitting in Gatsby's splendid car, winging their way over the Queensboro Bridge, it seems to Nick that the city is a Mecca, a shrine to capitalism and opportunity. 'The city seen from the ... Bridge is always the city seen for the first time, in its first wild promise of all the mystery and the beauty in the world' (p. 67). Nevertheless, juxtaposed against this mood of elation, is a reminder of man's limitations and fragile mortality in the image of the hearse. Nick gives voice to life's contradictions and irregularities when he acknowledges, 'anything can happen now ... anything at all' (p. 67) – including the phenomenon of Gatsby.

Nick's and Gatsby's relationships with women compared

At the end of this chapter, readers are invited to consider the differences between Nick and Jordan's affair and that of Gatsby and Daisy. The two relationships run parallel throughout the novel and present a marked contrast to each other. Unlike Gatsby, Nick does not delude himself. He becomes aware very early on of Jordan's shortcomings, but accepts, at least at first, the reality of 'this clean, hard, limited person, who dealt in universal scepticism' (p. 77).

Chapter V

When Nick returns to West Egg, he discovers Gatsby's house lit up like 'the World's Fair' (p. 79). Gatsby is restless and very anxious about organizing the meeting with Daisy. In a clumsy attempt to show his appreciation, he offers Nick a business opportunity, which Nick declines.

On the appointed day, Gatsby sends over someone to cut Nick's lawn; he also sends flowers. He arrives himself an hour early and waits, miserably, for Daisy. When her car pulls up, he disappears out the back way, only to reappear at Nick's front door, as if by accident. Initially the reunion does not go well. By this stage, Gatsby is so nervous that he can barely function, while Daisy is embarrassed and confounded by the unexpected meeting. In desperation, Nick leaves them alone for half an hour and waits in the garden. When he returns, the mood has altered dramatically. Their joy at rediscovering each other is palpable. Gatsby wants to show Daisy his house, so all three walk over for a tour. While Daisy admires the gardens, the architectural features, the possessions inside, Gatsby watches her hungrily and re-values everything 'according to the measure of response it drew from her well-loved eyes' (p. 88). By the time they arrive at his bedroom and go through his wardrobe, Daisy breaks down and cries, quite overcome.

The resumption of rain precludes further inspection of the grounds, so they spend the rest of the afternoon inside. They listen to Klipspringer, a house-guest of Gatsby's, play the piano. Nick asks about the photograph of an elderly man, whom Gatsby maintains was his best friend. The name, Dan Cody, sounds familiar. Finally, Nick leaves Daisy and Gatsby alone, totally absorbed in each other.

Gatsby's offer to augment Nick's income

Gatsby's offer to supplement Nick's modest income as a bond salesman in return for his help with Daisy, though well-meaning, betrays a crude, pragmatic streak. This is the man who 'does favours' for people in high places, the man who is used to buying his way out of trouble. Equally, Nick's response is revealing. There is no question in his mind of accepting the offer. We are reminded of his previous declaration that he is 'one of the few honest people that [he] has ever known' (p. 59).

Gatsby and Daisy re-united; Gatsby's emotional turmoil

The reunion between Gatsby and Daisy is poignant, funny, romantic, and ultimately sad. Though Nick narrates the sequence of events, it is Gatsby's emotional perspective that is the chapter's focus. We witness and share his initial torment, followed by the elation and wonder, which he experiences at Daisy's re-appearance. The mood of quiet serenity established at the end, as the lovers sit in the gathering darkness, oblivious to everything but each other, is a powerful antidote to the agitated state detailed at the beginning.

Gatsby has waited for the time when he will win back Daisy's love with such single-minded intensity that the actual fact of her presence has him 'running down like an overwound clock' (p. 89). Nick recognises the commitment and the energy that has gone into Gatsby's dream of reconciliation. He also recognises its limitations:

> 'There must have been moments even that afternoon when Daisy tumbled short of his dreams – not through her own fault, but because of the colossal vitality of his illusion. It had gone beyond her, beyond everything' (p. 92).

The Daisy Gatsby desires and loves

It will become evident that it is the *idea* of Daisy, rather than the real, fallible version, which Gatsby loves and wants. Daisy is representative of a world of beauty and elegance and money. Her availability is contingent on his entry into that world. In order to recapture her heart, Gatsby must prove himself worthy: hence the importance to him of showing her his house and his possessions. The shirts she cries over (p. 89) highlight this relationship between love and money, and are a symbol of the materialism which is integral to the success of his ambition.

Chapter VI

In order to refute the wild rumours that continue to fuel Gatsby's notoriety, Nick gives the reader part of the real story, as it was told to him much later. James Gatz was the son of poor, unsuccessful farm people from North Dakota. Discontented and ambitious, he had tried to make a living in various ways, all the while dreaming of a life of promise and luxury. At seventeen, he met Dan Cody, a millionaire several times over, who became his employer and mentor. For five years, they sailed the American seas in Cody's fabulous yacht, until the latter's death. Cody left Gatsby a legacy of twenty-five thousand dollars, but through the intervention of a jealous mistress, Gatsby received none of it. This is as much as we learn about Gatsby's past at this point. (pp. 94-96)

One Sunday afternoon, several weeks after the meeting with Daisy, Nick goes over to Gatsby's house. By coincidence, Tom Buchanan arrives on horseback with two friends. They come in for a drink. There is some talk of Gatsby joining them for dinner, though Tom disapproves of the idea, as indeed he disapproves of Gatsby. In the end, they leave without him.

The following Saturday evening, Tom accompanies Daisy to one of Gatsby's parties. Neither has a good time. Tom is rude and condescending. Daisy, although she is loyally determined to enjoy the splendour on offer, is profoundly offended by the crassness and vulgarity of West Egg. She is 'appalled by its raw vigour that chafed under the old euphemisms and by the too obtrusive fate that herded its inhabitants along a short-cut from nothing to nothing' (p. 103). After everyone leaves, Gatsby is tired and depressed, unhappily conscious that the occasion has not been a success. Nick tries to point out to him the impossibility of repeating the past, but Gatsby will have none of it. He confides his dreams to Nick and the chapter ends with a memory: a memory of Gatsby kissing Daisy's upturned mouth five years before, and, in so doing, sealing forever his restless destiny.

The significance of Dan Cody in Gatsby's life

When the young James Gatz first watches Dan Cody's splendid yacht drop anchor on Lake Superior, it represents 'all the beauty and glamour in the world' (p. 96). Up until this point, he has drifted without direction, sustained only by his imagination and the passionate belief that his destiny holds so much more. The relationship with Dan Cody provides Gatsby with the opportunity to realise that destiny. It is the springboard which gives him his education, unconventional, albeit appropriate, and exposes him, for the first time to a world of luxury and indulgence. It crystalises the image of the man he wants to be. Gatsby's concept of himself is ambitious, single-minded, and as far removed as possible from the mediocre reality of his childhood:

> The truth was that Jay Gatsby of West Egg, Long Island, sprang from his Platonic conception of himself. He was a son of God ... and he must be about His Father's business, the service of a vast, vulgar, and meretricious beauty (p. 95).

He literally reinvents himself.

The American Dream

The American Dream is a myth that has many parts. One of its most enduring elements is the belief that the individual can rise to great heights – in terms of wealth and often status – and the "rags to riches" stories are testimony to this. Gatsby's determination to win Daisy finds its basis in the belief that one person can single handedly overcome virtually insurmountable odds.

The 'American Dream' – the notion that anyone can achieve anything, as long as they want it enough and are prepared to work hard to attain it – finds expression in Gatsby's metamorphosis. However, a clue as to its flawed nature lies in the narrator's (Nick's? Fitzgerald's?) perception that Gatsby's image of himself is conceived as an immature and 'extravagantly ambitious' adolescent; ' ... he invented just the sort of Jay Gatsby that a seventeen-year-old boy would be likely to invent, and to this conception he was faithful to the end' (p. 95). Gatsby never digresses from the illusion that life can be determined, even manipulated, according to his aspirations. He remains unable to accommodate the irony that 'the rock of the world [is] founded securely on a fairy's wing' (p. 96). His desire to re-capture the past is a significant example. He is incredulous and dismissive of Nick's tentative suggestion that the past cannot be repeated. (p. 106) It is not enough that Daisy love him now, or even that she acknowledges regret for decisions wrongly made. He literally wants her to emotionally obliterate the life she has shared with Tom, so they can return to the point at which they first met, in order to start again. The expectation is as poignant as it is unreasonable.

East Egg/West Egg – the Buchanans/Gatsby

This is the chapter in which Gatsby's world and the world of the Buchanan's collide. East Egg, with its snobbery, its traditions, its sense of 'establishment' comes up against West Egg, with its brash, pretentious energy. Both 'old money' and 'new money' have rubbed shoulders before at Gatsby's parties, not always comfortably. At the first one which Nick attends, he finds himself with a group self-consciously mindful of their social superiority, 'East Egg condescending to West Egg and carefully on guard against its spectroscopic gaiety' (p. 46). In a supposedly egalitarian society, there are clear distinctions, even amongst the wealthy. Gatsby himself is oblivious to these distinctions. Even Nick forgets them for a while, 'I had ... grown to accept West Egg as a world complete in itself ... second to nothing because it had no consciousness of being so, and now I was looking at it again, through Daisy's eyes' (p. 100). However, with Tom sneering at her side, Daisy is painfully aware of the evening's shortcomings. Gatsby's guests, with their drunken antics and doubtful antecedents, set the tone. For all its lavishness, the party lacks class, and Daisy's emotional response to its careless vulgarity reflects the unwilling divide that exists between her and Gatsby.

Chapter VII

As a result of Daisy's disapproval, Gatsby holds no more parties. He dismisses his servants and replaces them with some contacts of Wolfshiem on whose discretion he can rely. He and Daisy continue to see each other.

Nick receives an invitation to have lunch with the Buchanans and, on the appointed day, he makes his way over to their house in searing heat. Gatsby and Jordan are also present. After meeting Tom and Daisy's little girl, the five of them sit down to a desultory lunch. The weather is stifling, and Nick is worried that a confrontation is looming between Gatsby and Tom. On a whim, Daisy suggests that they all go to town for the afternoon. She shares a look with Gatsby, which Tom intercepts and correctly interprets as an expression of love.

They exchange cars for the drive up to New York; Gatsby and Daisy drive Tom's coupe, and the other three go in Gatsby's car. Tom realises that Nick and Jordan already know about the relationship between Gatsby and Daisy. Barely controlling his temper, he claims to have done some digging into Gatsby's background. The car needs petrol, so Tom stops at Wilson's garage. Wilson is in a bad way. Though he does not suspect Tom, he has discovered that his wife is having an affair with someone, and the knowledge has made him physically ill. He announces his intention of taking Myrtle away and asks Tom to sell him his old car, as he needs the money. As they pull off, Nick becomes aware of Myrtle Wilson watching them with jealous intensity.

In an effort to escape the heat, the five go to the Plaza Hotel and engage a room, where they drink iced mint juleps and make half-hearted conversation. The tension between Tom and Gatsby finally explodes. Nick and Jordan listen unwillingly as the other three confront each other. Gatsby affirms that Daisy loves him, never loved Tom, and is leaving her marriage. Tom, though he acknowledges that he has behaved badly on occasions, insists that *he* loves Daisy and will take 'better care' of her from now on. To Gatsby's consternation, he forces from Daisy the admission that she did love him, once. With calculated brutality, he proceeds to discredit Gatsby, accusing him of bootlegging and other criminal activities. And with each accusation, Daisy becomes more frightened and remote, until it is evident that 'whatever intentions, whatever courage she had had, were definitely gone' (p. 128). They all start for home. This time, Gatsby drives his own car, accompanied by Daisy, while Tom, Jordan and Nick follow in Tom's coupe.

As they near the ash heaps, it becomes obvious there has been an accident. Myrtle Wilson has been knocked down and killed by a large, yellow car travelling at high speed from New York. The car did not stop. At the inquest, the principal witness testified that George Wilson and his wife had been arguing all afternoon. She had been locked upstairs, but had rushed out from the garage when she saw the 'death car' (p.131) approaching, 'waving her hands and shouting' (p. 130).

By the time Tom and the others arrive on the scene, there is little they can do. It dawns on the shocked Wilson that the car is the same one Tom was driving earlier in the day. Tom denies it is his vehicle and they leave hurriedly. Tom's angry assumption is that Gatsby is responsible for Myrtle's death.

When they return to the Buchanans', Tom invites Nick and Jordan inside for some supper, but Nick declines. He walks down to the gate to wait for his taxi and discovers Gatsby lurking in the garden. Gatsby admits that it was Daisy who was driving the car. While he obviously regrets the accident, it is Daisy's reaction and safety that preoccupies him. He intends to wait outside the house, 'all night, if necessary' (p. 137), in order to protect her from Tom. Concerned, Nick walks quietly back to check for himself. Through the pantry window, he observes the Buchanans sitting together, sharing a plate of cold chicken and some ale. 'There was an unmistakable air of natural intimacy about the picture, and anybody would have said that they were conspiring together' (p.138).

Death – metaphorical and literal

The oppressive heat with which this long, crucial chapter begins creates a mood of foreboding, a sense of something brewing out of control. When Nick arrives at the Buchanans' house for lunch, he is plagued by the lurid fantasy that murder is about to be committed. Throughout the meal, everyone is on edge, volatile emotions simmer just beneath the surface. When the confrontation finally occurs at the Plaza Hotel in New York, it *does* result in the metaphorical death of Gatsby's dream. Myrtle Wilson's literal death follows shortly after.

Daisy's wavering commitment to Gatsby

KEY POINT

Gatsby's inability to understand either Daisy herself or her situation is revealed clearly in this chapter. He expects her to reject the events of the past five years and to resume their relationship as though nothing has happened for her in the interim.

As Gatsby's loyalty, idealism and passion come up against Tom's 'hard malice', we become increasingly aware of the fragility of Daisy's commitment. The pressure put on her at this point by both her husband and her lover is acute. Tom and Gatsby, each in their own way, attempt to impose their will on her; Tom with bullying paternalism, Gatsby with impassioned urgency. Nevertheless the uncertainty of Daisy's response suggests that, despite dissatisfaction with her marriage and pleasure at the resumption of the relationship with Gatsby, she never really intended to leave Tom. Passive and fearful, she is incapable of facing the consequences of such an initiative. She simply wants to evade the issue. For his part, Gatsby has no understanding of and little sympathy for her dilemma. The reality of her life with Tom is a fact that he categorically denies; when he first meets her daughter, for example, he seems surprised at her actual existence. (Ironically, Daisy herself calls the child an 'absolute little dream' (p. 112.) What Gatsby demands of Daisy is that she also reject the past; it is inconceivable to him that she might have loved both him *and* Tom, or that the years she spent with her husband did not include periods of happiness and intimacy. It is a simplistic view of relationships which excludes any appreciation of the subtleties and complexities of the human heart.

Tom's reaction to Daisy's involvement with Gatsby

Unlike George Wilson, who becomes physically ill when he learns of his wife's adultery, Tom responds aggressively to a similar discovery. It comes as a profound shock that Daisy might love someone else, and in fact increases her value in his eyes. As a prized possession, he is determined to fight to retain her. By the time he has finished his attack on Gatsby, the latter's dream of a life with Daisy at its centre is dead, reduced to a 'presumptuous little flirtation' (p. 129).

Imagery of corruption and death

Note the abundance of imagery in this chapter which deals with corruption and death. The 'relentless beating' heat which forms the backdrop to the human drama being played out is not life-giving, but enervating, sapping individual will and promoting decay. The Sound (a long, wide ocean inlet) in front of the Buchanans' house is green and 'stagnant'. (p. 112) Jordan chides Daisy for being 'morbid' (p. 113), and later talks about 'overripe' fruit (p. 112). This reference is echoed in the description of the dead Myrtle, split open by the 'death car', in a grotesque parody of the sensuous vitality which she displayed in life (p. 131). Gatsby and Daisy, as a couple, are 'snapped out, made accidental, isolated, like ghosts' (p. 129). When Nick and the others leave the Plaza for the return journey, Nick realises that it is his thirtieth birthday, with its 'menacing' (p. 129) connotations of loneliness and apathy.

Careless driving becomes an important metaphor

There is considerable irony in the fact that Daisy, driving Gatsby's car, inadvertently kills her husband's mistress and, in so doing, seals her own lover's death warrant. Equally, Tom's whim in swapping cars for the journey to New York is instrumental in causing Myrtle's death. Thinking he is also driving the yellow car on the way back, she runs out frantically in front of it, in order to speak with him. Throughout the text, the damaging consequences of careless driving come up again and again, acting as a metaphor for irresponsible behaviour in general. The treacherous judgment shown by Daisy, both in terms of avoiding impact and then leaving the scene of the accident, represents the most critical loss of control depicted, and the most far-reaching.

Gatsby's useless sacrifice

The chapter concludes poignantly. When Nick discovers that Gatsby is prepared to take the blame for the accident, his feelings shift from disgust to support. However, it is borne home to him that the generosity of Gatsby's sacrifice is wasted. The picture of intimate collusion that he witnesses through the Buchanan's window, shocking under the circumstances, makes a mockery of Gatsby's anxious vigil. Nick walks away sadly, leaving him standing alone in the moonlight, 'watching over nothing' (p. 139).

Chapter VIII

Towards dawn, Gatsby returns to West Egg and Nick hurries over to speak to him. He tries to persuade Gatsby to go away for awhile, until things blow over, but the latter will not hear of it. This is the night that Gatsby tells Nick of his first meeting with Dan Cody. He also talks about Daisy. 'She was the first "nice" girl he had ever known' (p. 141). Rich and beautiful, she captured his heart. Daisy assumed that the young officer was from a similar background as herself and reciprocated his love. They shared a month of passion, before Gatsby was posted abroad. He distinguished himself on active service and was promoted to major. After the armistice, he was sent unwillingly to Oxford. Meanwhile, Daisy was finding the separation too difficult. She began to 'move again with the season' (p. 144), and the following spring, married Tom Buchanan. Gatsby was devastated. When he returned to the States, he made a miserable pilgrimage to Louisville, unable to reconcile himself to her loss.

Nick and Gatsby talk until dawn and then have breakfast together. As he is leaving, Nick calls to out to Gatsby that he is 'worth the whole damn bunch put together' (p. 146). Later that morning, Jordan rings Nick at work and suggests they meet. Tired and disillusioned, Nick puts her off. They both know their relationship is finished.

Back at garage, George Wilson is incoherent with grief. Friends sit with him for a while, but in the end, it is only his neighbour, Michaelis, who keeps him company and listens to the litany of insinuation and accusation. Wilson convinces himself that Myrtle's accident was deliberate murder and the man responsible – the driver of the yellow car – is the same man with whom she had been having an affair. Exhausted, Michaelis goes home for a sleep and when he returns, Wilson has set off alone, determined to find the guilty party. His investigations eventually lead him to Gatsby. By the time Nick returns anxiously to West Egg, he discovers his friend's body floating in the swimming pool. Wilson has shot and killed Gatsby, then himself. His own body lies nearby.

Links between Gatsby's ambition and his love for Daisy

Gatsby's reminiscences highlight the nexus between his ambition to make something of himself and Daisy's love. Part of Daisy's desirability is based on her membership to an exclusive world to which he desperately craves entry. At the same time, falling in love with her reinforces the imperative to better himself. Her beautiful house, with its cool mystery and suggestions of romance, is something to aspire to – he knows he is only there by 'a colossal accident' – but what makes it special is that Daisy lives there, and 'it was as casual a thing to her as his tent out at camp was to him' (p. 141). Wanting Daisy and wanting to be a part of her world become intertwined. In consummating their relationship, he discovers he has 'committed himself to the following of a grail' (p. 142) The religious imagery which describes his quest for Daisy's heart is significant. Winning her love becomes a spiritual ideal. The corrupting anomaly is that in order to do so, he must acquire the material wealth which provides entry into her domain. The image of Daisy, 'gleaming like silver, safe and proud above the hot struggles of the poor' (p. 142), encapsulates the interchangeable elements of Gatsby's dream.

Daisy's betrayal of Gatsby

Gatsby's final realisation that he has placed too much trust in Daisy's constancy is full of pathos. Floating in his pool, surrounded by evidence of his 'success', he waits for a phone call from her that never comes. However, Daisy's betrayal is part of a pattern. When she marries Tom Buchanan simply because she is too weak and indecisive to wait, it foreshadows her acceptance of his reassuring paternalism after Myrtle's death. Daisy is too dependant to assume a proactive role in her own life. 'She wanted her life shaped now, immediately – and the decision must be made by some force – of love, of money, of unquestionable practicality – that was close at hand' (p. 144). Whether Gatsby retains any of his illusions is unclear. Nick *does* recognise the emotional and spiritual death which losing them would involve. If that *were* the case, Gatsby 'must have felt that he had lost the old warm world, paid a high price for living too long with a single dream' (p. 153). Arguably, Gatsby would be left with nothing worth living for, merely an unwelcome existence, 'material without being real' (pp. 153-54).

Nick's friendship for Gatsby affirmed; Jordan rejected

It is at this late stage in their relationship that Nick declares his allegiance to Gatsby. Listening to Gatsby's story, sharing his confidences, Nick offers his friendship. His shout of affirmation as he leaves Gatsby, on the last morning they spend together, is a testament to that friendship. In many respects it has been a reluctant endorsement. Nick admits that he 'disapproved of him [Gatsby] from beginning to end' (pp. 146-47). Nevertheless, Nick can see that, despite the fallacies and broken trust which underpin Gatsby's illusion, it has its own worth and integrity, which sets him above the self-serving hypocrisy of the Buchanans' and their kind. In shifting his loyalties, Nick also rejects the relationship with Jordan. He is no longer able to overlook the insensitivities in her make-up which reflect a false, or at least a contrary, set of values. Ask yourself to what extent does Nick's judgement proclaim his own innocence?

'The eyes of God'

Finally, note how, in his shock and distress, George Wilson confuses the pale stare of Doctor T. J. Eckleburg with the eyes of God. Living under the shadow of the enormous billboard, Wilson has tried to convince his wayward wife that God witnesses and judges every human action. Once again, the notion that individuals are accountable for their behaviour is raised. However, in the light of subsequent events, Wilson's belief in a day of fair reckoning seems as much an illusion as Dr. Eckleburg's interest in human affairs.

Chapter IX

The next few days are a miserable blur from Nick's point of view. At the inquest, Myrtle's sister, Catherine, testifies that her sister was happily married and had never met Gatsby, so it is concluded that Wilson was 'deranged by grief' (p.155).

In the meantime, Nick assumes responsibility for the funeral arrangements. He tries to contact family and friends, but the only positive response comes from Gatsby's father. Henry C. Gatz, a 'solemn old man, very helpless and dismayed' (p.158), travels from Minnesota as soon as he reads of his son's death in the Chicago newspapers. The Buchanans have left town. Meyer Wolfshiem refuses to get involved. When Nick makes the trip to New York in order to persuade him to attend the funeral, he is sentimental about his first meeting with Gatsby, as a penniless, but impressive, young officer, just after the war. However, the 'friendship' does not extend to getting 'mixed up' with Gatsby's death (p. 157)

Henry Gatz is enormously proud of his son and somewhat in awe of Gatsby's achievements. He shows Nick an old novel which itemises the young Gatsby's resolutions on its back cover. It is evident that, even as a boy, Gatsby was bent on self-improvement. However, the funeral is a sorry affair. The only mourners are Nick, Mr. Gatz, a few servants, and the man with the owl-eyed glasses whom Nick met at one of Gatsby's parties. There is no word from Daisy.

Utterly disillusioned, Nick decides to return home to the Mid-West. Before he leaves, he arranges to meet Jordan Baker in order to say good-bye. She is still a little bitter at being 'thrown over' by him, a 'new experience' (p.168) for her. She reminds Nick of their conversation about careless drivers and accuses him of also being a 'bad driver'. Clearly she feels let down in her estimation of him.

Nick also encounters Tom Buchanan inadvertently one afternoon in New York. Tom confirms Nick's suspicion that it was he who had told George Wilson that Gatsby was responsible for his wife's death. Nick's anger gives way to melancholy; ' I shook hands with him; it seemed silly not to, for I felt suddenly as though I were talking to a child' (p. 170).

On Nick's last night at West Egg, he goes over to look at Gatsby's 'huge incoherent failure of a house' (p. 171). He reflects on the failure of Gatsby's dream and the ongoing struggle of human beings to shape for themselves some sense of purpose and destiny.

Gatsby's funeral

The contrast between Gatsby's ill-attended funeral and his parties is pathetic. Of the hundreds who used to take advantage of his hospitality throughout the summer, only one makes the effort to mourn his passing. The shallow indifference of Gatsby's guests is exemplified by Klipspringer. Going on a picnic is a greater priority than attending the funeral of the man who kept him for months. Presumably, he is now sponging off the people in Greenwich, just as he sponged off Gatsby. Gatsby's 'closest friend' (p.162) and business associate, Meyer Wolfshiem, while expressing profuse regret at Gatsby's death, refuses to leave New York. He rationalises this self-serving decision with the proverb, 'Let us learn to show our friendship for a man when he is alive and not after he is dead' (p. 163) .

But the most contemptible omission is Daisy. Nick telephones her 'instinctively and without hesitation' (p. 156) half an hour after finding Gatsby's body, only to be told that the Buchanans' have gone away. They have left no forwarding address, nor indicated to their servants when they will return. The assumption that they can simply leave trouble behind and move on with their lives is breathtakingly arrogant. When Nick subsequently runs into Tom Buchanan in New York, he is forced to acknowledge the fact that money and power provide exemption from the rules and constraints which operate for everyone else:

> They were careless people, Tom and Daisy – they smashed up things
> and creatures and then retreated back into their money or their vast
> carelessness, or whatever it was that kept them together, and let
> other people clean up the mess they had made...(p.170).

Daisy allows Gatsby to assume blame for her wrongdoing; the nobility of the gesture is taken for granted. Similarly, she allows Tom to take control afterwards; this absolves her from the necessity of confronting unpleasant consequences. She is willing to abandon her lover and lie to her husband (it seems doubtful whether she confesses the truth behind Myrtle's accident to Tom). The disparity between Daisy's moral cowardice and Gatsby's idealisation of her is profound.

Nick is left with the sense that he alone is on Gatsby's side, 'I began to have a feeling of defiance, of scornful solidarity between Gatsby and me against them all' (p. 157). He describes himself to Mr. Gatz as his son's close friend, but it becomes clear that he is indeed Gatsby's only friend. Gatsby's world has been full of selfish, superficial people, freeloaders and users, people who take what they can get and give nothing in return. Daisy and Tom, for all their snobbery and delusions of social superiority, are no better.

Gatsby's background and youthful naivety

The appearance of Henry Gatz is a reminder of how far, in the material sense, Gatsby has come. Gatsby's schedule of boyhood resolutions is revealing. The initiative and youthful ambition which leads him to organize his time-table and maximize his opportunities ultimately distance him from his own family, despite the resolve to be 'better to parents'. There is an endearing naivety in the list: Gatsby never outgrows his innocent faith in his ability to master his own destiny.

Nick's rejection of the East

Note Nick's reaction to the East after Gatsby's death. It takes on the distorted, nightmarish qualities of an El Greco painting. West Egg, in particular, presents a haunted, impersonal contrast to the cheerful familiarity of Nick's Middle West. He has come full circle and, once again, appreciates the value of family traditions, of continuity. Nick wonders if there is not 'some deficiency in common' which makes him, along with Gatsby, Jordan, and the Buchanans' 'subtly unadaptable to Eastern life' (p.167). Might this be true? Is Nick's return to the Mid-West an admission of defeat or an affirmation of more permanent, worthwhile values?

Consider also Nick's last meeting with Jordan. What does she mean when she accuses him of being a bad driver, instead of the 'rather honest, straightforward person' (p.168) she thought him to be? Are we to set any store by this, or is it merely hurt pride? Certainly in his refusal to continue the relationship for all the wrong reasons, Nick demonstrates integrity and self-awareness.

The final image: the continuity of people's illusions

The final beautiful passage evokes the image of Long Island as it must have appeared to the original Dutch sailors as an enchanted place of promise and challenge, hope and wonder. Nick draws a parallel between their response and Gatsby's, when he first identifies the green light at the end of Daisy's dock. He perceives Gatsby to be part of a pattern and muses on the continuity of people's illusions. Like Gatsby, their dreams will continue to elude them as long as they are unable to recognise the true foundation of human happiness, which is emotional and spiritual, rather than material.

CHARACTERS & RELATIONSHIPS

These studies discuss character development and factors that affect their key relationships. These are for your consideration to be used as catalyst for your own interpretations. Remember to support your ideas with evidence from the text.

Jay Gatsby

Many readers have expressed the criticism that Gatsby is a difficult character to understand and come to terms with. He remains an enigmatic, shadowy figure throughout the novel. Fitzgerald's correspondence with his editor suggests that this was, in fact, precisely the writer's intention. Our view of Gatsby is filtered through the screen of Nick's perceptions, and Nick's response to him is in a constant state of flux. As he comments at one point, ' it was like skimming hastily through a dozen magazines' (p. 65). The ambiguity that surrounds Gatsby is also reinforced by the structure of the novel, which moves back and forth in time, rationing out truths and half-truths, rumour and innuendo, in a deliberately confusing and contradictory fashion. It is up to Nick, and the reader, to sift through this information in order to arrive at the truth.

In any case, Gatsby is a chameleon. The first night that Nick makes his acquaintance, he is mindful of the contradictions which seem to present themselves. Gatsby is courteous and self-effacing. His smile, like Daisy's voice, is a rare, seductive tool. Just as the essence of Daisy's charm resides in her voice, so does Gatsby's in his smile. Once it vanishes, Nick realises he is 'looking at an elegant young rough-neck, a year or two over thirty, whose elaborate formality of speech just missed being absurd' (p. 49). Nick's original, well-disposed impression of the man is challenged by an intuition that Gatsby has somehow fabricated an identity for himself. This meeting highlights the two sides of Gatsby's public persona. Without the smile, he is de-mystified; Jay Gatsby reverts to James Gatz.

That smile is one of Gatsby's tickets out of the poverty of the Mid-West farming belt. As a boy, Gatsby's youthful enterprise and initiative are encapsulated in his schedule; the list is as eclectic as it is ambitious.

His association with Dan Cody enables him to exploit his charm (he discovers 'that people liked him when he smiled', p. 96) and exposes him to the world of wealth and privilege to which he aspires. By the time he is on his own, 'the vague contour of Jay Gatsby had filled out to the substantiality of a man' (p. 97). Gatsby exemplifies the concept of the self-made man. He has energy and a passionate belief in his own destiny. He has the valuable ability to make people like him (Meyer Wolfshiem recognises and puts to use his 'fine-appearing, gentlemanly' qualities, p. 162). Moreover his war service is testimony to his courage and leadership. These attributes are subsequently diverted into corrupt, but effective, channels in terms of raising his status in the world.

It is his relationship with Daisy that provides a focus for his ambition. The memory, which Gatsby shares with Nick, where he attempts to, put into words the transcendental experience of kissing her and irrevocably wedding 'his unutterable visions to her perishable breath' (p.107) evokes the genesis of his dream. Fitzgerald's prose conveys a mood, that is elusive and dream-like, yet resonates with intensity. Gatsby invests so much in this moment, it takes on a spiritual value: 'At his lip's touch she blossomed for him like a flower and the incarnation was complete' (p.107). Gatsby is aware of the interrelationship between his love for Daisy and his material ambitions. When, in response to Nick's inarticulate attempt to pinpoint the attraction of Daisy's voice, he says, 'Her voice is full of money' (p. 115), it perceptively sums up the essence of its charm for him and, by extension, the fascination of Daisy herself. Her wealth, social position, beauty and elegance are all irresistibly intertwined.

Gatsby's capacity to reject reality when it no longer accords with his vision of himself or the world ultimately precipitates his downfall. Repudiating the mediocrity of his boyhood in North Dakota, burying James Gatz and re-inventing himself as Jay Gatsby, capitalising on opportunities presented by Dan Cody and Meyer Woflshiem – all of these accomplishments involve formidable single-mindedness. However, it becomes evident that his determination to imprison Daisy in a moment in time nearly five years before, and return to that same point with her, regardless of all that has occurred in the interim, is an obsessive delusion.

Notwithstanding the difficulties implicit in turning back the clock, Gatsby is blind to the specific realities of Daisy's character and position. In this sense, he retains an innocence of heart and purpose which Nick cannot help but applaud. Like other great dreamers of literature, Don Quixote, and the like, the impossibility of his quest does not detract from the idealism which underpins it. Flawed though the dream may be, it is nevertheless a heroic failure. Whether Gatsby is a noble or pathetic figure is, of course, one of the questions you must determine for yourself. Nor can you ignore the tension which exists between Gatsby's corruption – the ruthless criminal activity which has spearheaded his wealth – and his 'incorruptible dream'.

Nick Carraway

Like Fitzgerald himself, Nick is a Mid-Westerner. While his family do not possess the kind of wealth the Buchanans flaunt, his background is solidly affluent, grounded in tradition and enterprise. Nick's great-uncle started up the wholesale hardware business that his father still carries on. The Carraways are clannish, with strong family traditions – prep school – Ivy League university. Nick acknowledges he is 'a little complacent from growing up in the Carraway house in a city where dwellings are still called through decades by a family's name' (p.167). What might have been a traumatic aberration – the experience of war – is 'enjoyable', but alters his perception of the conservative, parochial world of his youth. He comes East to make his fortune; to capitalise on the challenges and opportunities of New York. In this sense, he is linked from the onset with Gatsby, as a modern-day adventurer, an heir-apparent to those Dutch sailors whose spirit he evokes in the final chapter. When he first arrives at West Egg, he quickly becomes a 'pathfinder, an original settler' (p.9). Life is 'beginning over again' (p. 10). *The Great Gatsby* traces Nick's journey of discovery. Arguably, the central focus of the narrative is Nick's attempt to understand and come to terms with his experiences in the East, particularly his relationship with Gatsby.

The duality of Nick's role, both narrator *and* character in his own right, is finely balanced. Recounting events a year later, with the value of hindsight, enables him to superimpose his expanded vision on the narrative. Therefore he starts off with a conclusion, 'Gatsby turned out all right at the end' (p.8), and works backwards. Nick early establishes the credentials which will give his voice moral authority; he is honest, cautious, tolerant, wary of making snap judgements. Natural scepticism and a sense of irony encourage him to sit back and observe. At the same time, his emotional detachment distances him from other characters, at least at first. He has extricated himself from a relationship back home, 'I had no intention of being rumoured into marriage' (p. 24); then has a short affair with a girl in Jersey City, but lets it 'blow quietly away' at her brother's intervention (p. 57). Nor does he take up Daisy on her offer to 'fling' him together with Jordan. That relationship seems to occur more by accident than design: 'For a while I lost sight of [her], and then in mid-summer I found her again' (p. 58). Again, Nick is not in love, though he does feel 'a sort of tender curiosity' (p. 58). At this point, he describes himself as 'slow-thinking and full of interior rules that act as breaks on my desires' (p. 59). This unwillingness, or inability to commit himself emotionally is in marked contrast to the more proactive role he assumes later on. He moves from observing life to actively participating in it.

What of Nick's relationship with Daisy? If he is not in love with her himself, as some critics have suggested, he is certainly appreciative of her charm and physical attractions, including her magical voice. This is emphasised at their first meeting and reinforced throughout. While Nick protests that Daisy makes him feel 'uncivilized' (p. 17), in fact he appears more on her wavelength than Tom. They converse in the same sophisticated banter, and Nick quickly becomes her confidante. She is quite willing to accept the invitation to come to his house alone: 'Are you in love with me?' (p. 83).

Even so, he is capable of viewing Daisy objectively. That first evening, as Nick is drawn into her confidence, he also becomes aware of a disconcerting duplicity: 'The instant her voice broke off, ceasing to compel my attention, my belief, I felt the basic insincerity of what she had said' (p.22).

However, it is Nick's relationship with Gatsby that ultimately defines his relationship to the other characters in the text. At first Nick maintains the same ironic distance towards his flamboyant neighbour as he does towards everyone else. Gradually he becomes sympathetic to the commitment and romantic vision, which has motivated Gatsby since first meeting Daisy. Flawed though Gatsby's dream may be, it nonetheless represents something heroic and enriching in the human psyche. By the end of the novel, Nick retains some of his ambivalence towards Gatsby, but makes an emotional commitment which inevitably leads to moral judgements. The most notable is a condemnation of the Buchanans' and their empty, self-serving world. Whereas, at the beginning of his relationship with Jordan, Nick says 'Dishonesty in a woman is a thing you never blame deeply' (pp. 58-59), ultimately he *does* blame Daisy for her dishonesty and moral cowardice. Readers are invited to share in this process of judgement and identify with Nick's conclusions. Nevertheless, it is vital to appreciate that he too has his own biases and limitations. You must ask yourself how accurate is Nick's perception of reality; in particular, how reliable is his assessment of Gatsby?

Daisy Buchanan

Daisy Buchanan is represented to the reader almost exclusively through the eyes of Nick and Gatsby. Both romanticise her and it becomes clear, as the novel progresses, that the real version falls tragically short of their expectations. Nick appreciates, as do all of the men who know her, her beauty and charm; 'Her face was sad and lovely with bright things in it, bright eyes and a bright passionate mouth ... ' (p. 14). He refers to the 'singing compulsion' of her voice on a number of occasions; its musicality is a potent weapon in the armoury of her charm. When Daisy is reunited with Gatsby, Nick wonders if she might not have difficulty in living up to the 'colossal vitality' (p.92) of Gatsby's illusion. He concludes it is her voice which holds him most, 'with its fluctuating, feverish warmth, because it couldn't be over-dreamed – that voice was a deathless song' (p. 93).

Daisy is circumscribed by this emphasis on her physical allure and desirability. The pedestal on which she is placed by Gatsby and Nick, and Tom to a certain extent, (for despite his infidelity, she is still a prized possession, far superior to his 'women') arises out of her beauty and social position. She is 'the king's daughter, the golden girl' (p. 115). From the reader's point of view, she is an elusive character, existing primarily as an embodiment of men's fantasies, rather than a thinking, feeling woman in her own right. In fact, her conversation is frivolous, often banal. The few ideas she initiates, as opposed to the times when she merely responds to those around her, reveal a rather glib cynicism which nevertheless alludes to constraints of gender and class. The pronouncement that 'the best thing a girl can be in this world [is] a beautiful little fool' (p. 22) is the most obvious example.

At the same time, Daisy is essentially a weak, passive woman who relies on other more forceful individuals to make decisions for her. She marries Tom Buchanan, rather than wait for Gatsby, and indeed is happy with him for a time because he is just such a man. Equally, it is doubtful if the love affair with Gatsby would have even got off the ground had she not made the assumption, and had he not let her believe, that 'he was fully able to take care of her' (p. 142). The same phrase is echoed by Tom at the confrontation at the Plaza Hotel: 'I'm going to take better care of you from now on' (p. 127). After Myrtle Wilson's death, she is protected from liability by Gatsby *and* Tom. Implicit in any relationship Daisy has is this expectation, and need, to be taken care of. Her spoilt, privileged existence has ill-prepared her for independence.

It is the selfish cowardice of Daisy's actions which ultimately indicts her in Nick's eyes. The fact that she does not even acknowledge Gatsby's death by word or deed is inexcusable under the circumstances. Nick comes to the bitter realisation that the Buchanans of this world inevitably present a united front in times of crisis. Insulated by their money, they are rarely held accountable for the suffering they cause and the damage they perpetrate.

Tom Buchanan

First impressions of Tom Buchanan are over-ridingly negative. Words such as 'hard', 'supercilious', 'arrogant', 'aggressively', 'cruel', feature in Nick's opening description. His body language, 'standing with his legs apart' (p. 12), asserts his inclination to dominate those with whom he comes in contact. Enormous wealth has made him powerful; limited intellectual capacity and a spoilt, bullying nature results in frequent abuse of this power. Nick has known him since university days at New Haven, where he distinguished himself playing football. Nick perceptively notes Tom's lack of direction once his football days were over; he is 'one of those men who reach such an acute limited excellence at twenty-one that everything afterwards savours of anti-climax' (p. 11). His arrogance and belligerence make him unpopular with his peers, though Nick senses that Tom would, at least, value his approval.

Tom is much given to the grand gesture. When he marries Daisy, he comes down to Louisville with a huge entourage and hires out a whole floor of the city's best hotel. His wedding present to her is a prohibitively expensive string of pearls. He comes East from Chicago 'in a fashion that rather took your breath away' (p. 11), complete with a string of polo ponies. These ostentatious displays of wealth are essentially ego-driven. In his own way, Tom is just as liable to the flamboyance he criticises Gatsby for.

Tom has been unfaithful to Daisy since the beginning of their marriage. His taste seems to run to women outside his own social class (chambermaids, Myrtle Wilson), presumably because it is easier to dominate them, but also because it enables him to rationalise his behaviour. The way in which he compartmentalises his relationships is evident when he refuses to allow his mistress to use Daisy's name. Ironically, Tom sees himself as representing all that is fine and upstanding about civilised society. His references to the pseudo-scientific racist propaganda of *The Rise of the Coloured Empires*, and the readiness with which he quotes the sanctity of family life and the need to preserve 'white' values when he feels under threat from Gatsby, is both ludicrous and disturbing.

Tom's pragmatism and total lack of imagination make him an interesting contrast to Gatsby. Unlike Gatsby, he has few romantic pretensions. His view of the world is a literal one. Yet for all Tom's outward success, he is a restless and discontented man, whose life lacks any sort of spiritual or emotional core.

Jordan Baker

Nick's first impressions of Jordan are of a studied self-sufficiency. She is sitting with Daisy on a couch, very still, and appears to be balancing some sort of object on her chin. Despite her affectation, Nick finds her attractive; she has a slender, boyish figure, and a 'wan, charming, discontented face' (p. 16). She is an independent young woman; according to Tom, too independent. He deplores the way in which she 'runs around the country' (p. 23). Her background and social position are allied with Daisy's; they went to school together in Louisville and have remained friends. This relationship enables Jordan to fill in the narrative gaps for Nick, for those times when neither he nor Gatsby is present.

Nick discovers, in the course of the evening, that Jordan is a well-known golf champion, and recalls that he has heard a 'critical, unpleasant story' (p. 23) about her, though the details elude him. When he knows her better and witnesses first-hand evidence of her capacity for deception, he remembers the story was to do with her cheating in a tournament. The poised, contemptuous front she presents to the world disguises an incurable dishonesty. Jordan is unable to endure being placed at any kind of disadvantage and Nick perceives that she instinctively avoids 'clever, shrewd men' (p. 58) as they would be more likely to uncover her dishonesty. Ironically, she seems unaware that Nick sees through her facade, though she admits she can be 'careless' (p. 168).

Jordan's cool, sardonic manner makes for some black humour on occasions – especially with regard to Tom. When the latter angrily asserts that he has conducted an investigation into Gatsby's affairs, she innocently inquires if he has been to a medium. (p. 116) Later she interrupts his impassioned references to intermarriage between black and white to point out, 'We're all white here' (p. 124).

Nick is flattered by Jordan's interest in him and responds to the initiative she takes regarding their relationship. If, as he maintains to the reader, her dishonesty makes no difference to him, then why do they finally separate? After the confrontation at the Plaza Hotel, Nick seems to derive reassurance from his intimacy with Jordan, and there is a sense of solidarity between them which excludes the others: 'But there was Jordan beside me, who, unlike Daisy, was too wise ever to carry well-forgotten dreams from age to age ... the formidable stroke of thirty died away with the reassuring pressure of her hand' (p. 129). Myrtle Wilson's accident is the turning point. Nick is unable to rationalise her apparent indifference to the tragedy. Rightly or wrongly, Jordan is compromised in Nick's eyes by her association with the Buchanans. His response at their last meeting; 'angry', 'half in love' and 'tremendously sorry' (p. 169) sums up their complicated and ambivalent relationship.

Myrtle Wilson

Myrtle Wilson is a coarse, rather foolish woman, discontented in her marriage and bitterly disappointed with her husband. She despises George Wilson and is convinced that she has married beneath herself. Tom Buchanan, on the other hand, accords with her ideal of what a 'real' man should be; he is wealthy, confident, assertive, powerful. According to her sister, Catherine, Tom is 'the first sweetie she ever had' (p 37), although given the way in which Catherine lies at the inquest in order to protect Myrtle's reputation, this may not be true. The relationship would appear to be based on mutual sexual gratification. Myrtle exudes a sensuality which a womanizer like Tom would find hard to resist – ' ... there was an immediately perceptible vitality about her as if the nerves of her body were continually smouldering' (p. 28). Through Tom, Myrtle is vicariously living her fantasy of social betterment. Their apartment in New York, stocked as it is with tasteless possessions impulsively and indiscriminately purchased, is a showcase for her crude aspirations. It also symbolically defines the exact parameters of the relationship.

Myrtle deludes herself as to the extent of Tom's commitment. The demanding insistence with which she intrudes into the Buchanans' world, via the telephone, ('this fifth guest's shrill metallic urgency' (p. 21), her determination to be on an equal footing with Daisy in Tom's estimation, reveals her underlying desperation. It is the expectation or hope that Tom will somehow rescue her from Wilson which results in her frantic attempt to stop Gatsby's car, and her shocking death. Despite her limitations, it is difficult not to feel some sympathy for her predicament.

Meyer Wolfshiem

Meyer Wolfshiem is thought to have been based on the character of Arnold Rothstein, a notorious underworld figure who may or may not have 'fixed' the World Baseball Series of 1919, though there is little doubt that he knew of it and profited by it. Wolfshiem is an unattractive character with 'tiny eyes', hair growing out of his nostrils (p. 69), and table manners of a 'ferocious delicacy' (p. 69). For all his sentimentality, he is a ruthless, clever criminal. Having played with the faith of fifty million people with 'the single-mindedness of a burglar blowing a safe' (p. 71), he is too wily to be imprisoned. Gatsby clearly admires his cunning. Their long association not only underscores the fact that Gatsby's source of wealth owes a great deal to this dubious partnership, it also reveals Gatsby's own opportunistic, amoral streak. When Nick has lunch with the two of them in New York, he is disconcerted by the offhand references to other underworld characters. His assumption that Wolfshiem is a dentist – what kind of a man wears human molars as cuff links? (p. 70) – provides a moment of bleak humour. Wolfshiem's cowardly and hypocritical refusal to attend Gatsby's funeral, for fear that he might somehow be compromised, places his relationship with his 'friend' in grim perspective. Basically, the two men have made use of each other: the world they share is a callous, unpredictable one with little room for loyalty or compassion.

George Wilson

George Wilson is one of the 'ash-grey men' who live and work in the 'valley of ashes' (p. 26). A total failure as far as his wife is concerned, he runs a garage, eking out a barren, apathetic existence. Spiritless, anaemic, utterly worn-out by life, he is the kind of man whom people take advantage of, and then feel contempt for. Myrtle has decided that he isn't fit to lick her boots: she is appalled by the fact that he even had to borrow the suit he was married in. Patterns of imagery surrounding him reinforce the picture of a man with no life of his own – a sort of living ghost suffering a premature death: 'He was his wife's man and not his own' (p. 130); Myrtle walks through him 'as if he were a ghost' (p. 28). As Wilson stalks Gatsby at the end, he is a 'poor ghost', reduced to an 'ashen, fantastic figure' (p. 154).

Yet Wilson loves his wife and is devastated by her infidelity. Interestingly, he is more inclined to blame her lover than Myrtle herself. To his neighbour's surprise, Wilson behaves with uncharacteristic assertiveness in locking his wife above the garage and trying to force her to accompany him out West. The murder of Gatsby demonstrates the desperate lengths to which this mild, ineffectual man is prepared to go to redeem some measure of self-respect.

THEMES & ISSUES

The American Dream

Enshrined in American culture is the conviction that men, and women, are masters of their own destiny. Regardless of the circumstances of their birth, the 'American Dream' argues that individuals can achieve whatever it is they set their minds to, with effort and determination. Historically, the United States has been seen as a land of opportunity. At the end of the novel, Nick tries to imagine how the New World must have appeared to the Dutch sailors who first sighted it. Long Island 'flowered' before them:

> … for a transitory enchanted moment man must have held his breath in the presence of this continent, compelled into an aesthetic contemplation he neither understood nor desired, face to face for the last time in history with something commensurate to his capacity for wonder (p. 171).

These men were concerned with exploration and exploitation. The vast richness and beauty of the continent before them promised untold wealth and opportunity. The pioneers who followed were similarly bent on maximizing their chances in an environment, where the land itself and the prevailing political climate encouraged a spirit of entrepreneurialism. The old constraints and inequalities of European society were left behind. Ideals such as freedom and democracy hoped to destroy past injustices and promote an egalitarian society which afforded wealth and success to those who wanted it enough and were prepared to work hard to attain it. American folklore abounds with inspiring stories of individuals who started with nothing and rose to prominence in their world, or overcame great odds to achieve their goals.

Gatsby's struggle is therefore part of a cultural tradition, representative of this belief that the power of will can realise fortunes and transform individual circumstances. His youthful list of 'General Resolves' is an earnest attempt to articulate those qualities which will enable him to realise his destiny – industry, initiative, organisation, self-discipline, frugality – and echoes the advice of Benjamin Franklin to aspiring young men of the eighteenth century. However, Nick Carraway's advice from *his* father highlights one of the crucial fallacies undercutting the American Dream. It is a cold reality that not everyone is born with the same advantages. Nick concedes that 'a sense of the fundamental decencies is parcelled out unequally at birth' (p.7), and by inference, so is education, intelligence, material benefits, and so forth. This means that, in practice, it is often very difficult for individuals to transcend disadvantage and poverty. Jay Gatsby does it, though the avenues open to him are limited, and in availing himself of the opportunities which do present themselves, he is compromised in the eyes of more established wealth. As far as Tom Buchanan and his peers are concerned, he is just 'some big bootlegger', 'Mr. Nobody from Nowhere' (p. 123). On the one hand, Gatsby embodies the ideal of the self-made man, having risen from obscurity to wealth through his ambition; on the other, he typifies its limitations. The entrepreneurial spirit which sees him buy up side-street drugstores and sell grain alcohol over the counter is a distortion of the values expressed in his schedule. Moreover, when Tom destroys Gatsby's credibility in Daisy's eyes, it becomes evident that money alone does not provide entry into their world. The egalitarian ideals of the Founding Fathers underestimated society's instinct for classifying itself into hierarchies. Tom's inherited wealth gives him an entrenched power and a perceived social status which Gatsby cannot hope to emulate.

The Great Gatsby examines the way in which the American ideal of realising individual destiny, and the optimism and energy which are fundamental to this ideal, have become debased and confused with the pursuit of wealth. This process, in turn, can brutalize those unwilling, to operate within reasonable ethical boundaries. Dan Cody, Gatsby's mentor, is one such individual, who has ruthlessly exploited the resources of the land for his own profit. Nick summarizes him as an ugly character whose dissipated and unscrupulous lifestyle is a caricature of the pioneering model:

> I remember the portrait of him up in Gatsby's bedroom, a grey, florid man with a hard, empty face – the pioneer debauchee, who during one phase of American life brought back to the Eastern seaboard the savage violence of the frontier brothel and saloon (p. 97).

Cody has made millions through transactions in gold, silver and copper. Nevertheless, he represents the American dream reduced to its lowest common denominator.

Equally, New York is a modern frontier and affords ample opportunity for those with few scruples to make a killing. Gatsby's parties, for example, see 'hungry' young Englishmen trying to ingratiate themselves with prosperous Americans, 'agonizingly aware of the easy money in the vicinity and convinced that it was theirs for a few words in the right key' (p. 43). Nick Carraway resists the temptation to do the same. His ambition to make something of himself in the East does not extend to capitalising on the relationship with Gatsby. The rejection of Gatsby's offer to 'pick up a nice bit of money' in his 'confidential' side-line (p. 80) sets Nick above the acquisitiveness of other characters. This caution proves well-founded. Gatsby's 'gonnegtions' carry their risks, as Tom's friend, Walter Chase, discovers to his cost, and the sinister phone-call taken by Nick after Gatsby's death affirms.

Reality and illusion

The Great Gatsby raises the question as to whether or not individuals who have dreams, or illusions, which become all-encompassing are to be applauded or derided. Is it preferable to be a dreamer or a realist? Does Gatsby's willful determination to recreate the past with Daisy render him a deluded fool, or does the 'colossal vitality of his illusion' (p. 92) confer on him a substance and a worth – a nobility even – which sets him apart from other characters in the novel? Nick believes this to be the case and most readers are predisposed to accept this value judgment. Even so, to what extent is Nick himself being realistic in his endorsement of Gatsby's position?

The disparity between what is real and what is illusion is one of the critical issues in the text. The indifferent eyes of Dr. T. J. Eckleburg are confused with the eyes of God by a despairing George Wilson. Recurring images of 'eyes' and 'ways of seeing' remind the reader of the variations in individual perception of reality. The persona of Jay Gatsby is, in itself, a construct, a mythic creature of James Gatz' imagination. Gatsby's world, glamorous, lavish, and larger-than-life, evokes mystery and is heavily reliant on illusion. His stories, a little of the truth married to extravagant doses of fantasy, conjure up fabulous possibilities for Nick; 'I saw the skins of tigers flaming in his palace on the Grand Canal; I saw him opening a chest of rubies to ease, with their crimson-lighted depths, the gnawings of his broken heart' (p. 65-66). Gatsby's parties are, similarly, a magical illusion, designed to create an effect, but the 'caravansary' falls in 'like a card house' at Daisy's disapproval (p. 109).

The enduring image Nick has of his neighbour is one of isolation; Gatsby is inevitably alone, even in the frenzied context of his own parties. He is emotionally distanced from the world by his intense inner life. When he buys the mansion across the bay from the Buchanans' property, the green light at the end of Daisy's dock assumes the significance of a beacon. It is a tangible reminder of Daisy's presence in the world and a symbol of hope. For nearly five years, he has cherished her memory and worked towards the moment when they will be re-united. Moreover, he has convinced himself that she waits for him with the same anticipation. Marrying Tom was an aberration, a 'terrible mistake' which only occurred because he, Gatsby, was poor and Daisy was tired of waiting for him. Gatsby seems oblivious as to how inadequate this reveals her to be. His conception of her is romantic and idealised: her undeniable loveliness, 'the youth and mystery that wealth imprisons and preserves' (p. 142), have conspired to enthrall and inspire him. At the Plaza Hotel, he insists to Tom: ' in her heart she never loved anyone except me' ... 'both of us loved each other all that time ... and you didn't know ... I used to laugh sometimes ... to think that you didn't know' (p. 125). However, this kind of wish-fulfillment has nothing to do with the reality of the frightened woman who begs her husband to rescue her from the messy emotional scene which has been enacted on her behalf, and return her to the security of the life they share.

How well did Gatsby really know Daisy? Their affair was in fact very short – a 'month of love' (p. 143). The mutual closeness which appears to characterise the lovers' last afternoon together, before Gatsby is posted overseas, suggests a relationship of some depth. Nevertheless, this is still

Gatsby's version, as he relates it to Nick. Daisy's *actions*, her need to have her life determined and settled, her unwillingness to mark time, convey a different impression. Gatsby's understanding of Daisy's worth is a fantasy, based in part on the superficial attractions of the girl before him, but also on her symbolic value as a prize of great worth. Is Gatsby ever able to admit the truth to himself ? Nick believes that, had he done so, Gatsby would have been robbed of the central focus which gave *his* life meaning. This begs the question, is the world of illusion richer than reality? Gatsby appears to possess something precious and valuable by virtue of his very denial of reality that seems preferable to the inner sterility of his counterparts. Disillusionment brings spiritual impoverishment: without the dream, he is left with a 'new world, material without being real' (pp. 153-54).

Borrowed time

It has been argued that the twentieth century began with the First World War. It was this event, more than anything else, which changed people's lives and redefined their perception of the world. The linchpins of the past could no longer be relied on. Faith, spiritual ideals and traditional values were called into question. The devastation of the war generated a pessimism and an overwhelming feeling of confusion which were subsequently explored by writers and artists of the period. *The Great Gatsby* examines the spiritual malaise and moral bankruptcy of a generation that has lost direction, emotionally and figuratively.

It is apparent that there are few happy people in the novel. Fitzgerald presents us with a cross-section of society; on the face of it, these individuals have little in common. However, the lifestyles of the Buchanans and the Wilsons, so different superficially, are each characterised by a sense of futility and lack of purpose. By contrast, Gatsby, for all his illusions, at least has something to believe in. The Buchanans exemplify the truism that money cannot buy contentment. Bored, disaffected, they fill their days with empty plans and frivolous gestures. Daisy's *ennui* is, in part, a fashionable pose, bound up with her identity as a rich, spoilt young woman, but there is also an underlying anguish when she expresses her disgust at life to Nick: ' You see I think everything's terrible anyhow ... Everybody thinks so – the most advanced people' (p.22). Tom Buchanan is too arrogant and too complacent to articulate any dissatisfaction with his position. Nevertheless, Nick detects his restlessness; 'I felt that Tom would drift on forever seeking, a little wistfully, for the dramatic turbulence of some irrecoverable football game' (p.12).

Gatsby's parties, and the climate in which they are received, are significant. We see that they are merely extravagant forums for self-indulgence on the part of social parasites who behave as if there is no tomorrow. The facade of glamour and gaiety masks a reckless disregard for past conventions, and, indeed, each other.

The 'valley of ashes' (p.26) offers the most potent symbol of despair and alienation in the novel. The landscape is dead; the people who dwell there are living ghosts. Fitzgerald is sympathetic to the underprivilege of people like the Wilsons. While he is acutely aware of the ways in which money can sour and corrupt, he also demonstrates how wretched existence can be without it. George Wilson, literally, 'doesn't know he's alive' (p. 29).

QUESTIONS & ANSWERS

Sample exam questions

1 ' .... it is what preyed on Gatsby, what foul dust floated in the wake of his dreams that temporarily closed out my interest in the abortive sorrows and short-winded elations of men' (p.8). Who, or what, is responsible for Gatsby's death?

2 Jay Gatsby and Nick Carraway are two sides of the one coin. Discuss.

3 While writing *The Great Gatsby*, Fitzgerald maintained that the female characters are subordinate: ' .... the book contains no important woman character.' Do you consider this is true?

4 Discuss ways in which two or three important images and/or symbols are used in the novel.

5 ' .... life is much more successfully looked at from a single window' (p.10). Do you think the novel ultimately affirms or refutes this observation of Nick's?

6 How 'great' is Gatsby?

7 *The Great Gatsby* depicts a society which exists in a state of confusion and moral chaos. Discuss.

8 'They're a rotten crowd,' I shouted across the lawn. 'You're worth the whole damn bunch put together.' Do you agree with Nick's appraisal of Gatsby?

9 'Daisy's decision to stay with Tom Buchanan reveals moral cowardice. In the end Gatsby is better than people like Daisy'. Do you agree?

Analysing a sample question

3 ' ... life is much more successfully looked at from a single window.' Do you think the novel ultimately affirms or refutes this observation of Nick's?

Nick's epigram suggests that individuals who view life in a 'black-and-white' way, uncluttered by too many shades of grey, are more successful than those who don't. Do you consider that the novel supports this idea?

Are the lives of such individuals likely to be easier, happier? If so, why? Try not to define success too superficially. *The Great Gatsby* offers us several examples of material success. What about the success which comes from worthwhile relationships, emotional growth, self-awareness, and so forth?

Jay Gatsby is your obvious starting point. His vision of the world is absolutely focused. All of his formidable energies and talents have been channelled into winning Daisy back: this is the only thing of true importance in his life. What sacrifices and compromises has this ambition necessitated? Do you regard him as a failure because his dream proves ultimately unattainable or does his single-mindedness give him a substance and integrity which the other characters lack? Arguably, it is precisely his unwillingness, or inability, to see beyond his objective which precipitates his downfall. Note his refusal to listen to Nick when the latter tries to suggest the impossibility of repeating the past. At what point does a sense of purpose deteriorate into stubborn myopia?

Examine the way in which the other characters perceive the world and the effect of this. Nick's flexibility and tolerance enable him to move from a position of scepticism in his dealings with Gatsby, to admiration. He moves also from an ingenuous excitement at the life offered by the East to a wiser appreciation of its pitfalls. On the other hand, Tom Buchanan certainly exemplifies the principle of viewing life through a single window. He is pragmatic, ruthless and literal-minded. Should we regard this as a strength or a limitation? In the eyes of the world, Tom is the most 'successful' character in the novel. What do you think?

This topic raises a number of questions to do with the characters' worth and effectiveness. You are asked to take a position, and either agree or disagree with the statement, though a reasonable case could be argued either way. Remember to illustrate your point of view with detailed evidence from the text.

VITAL EXAM STRATEGIES

The following strategies are designed to assist you in revising your texts for the exam.

- Know your text thoroughly. There is actually no way to short-circuit this fundamental aspect of your revision. You *cannot* have read, or viewed, the texts too often. Study guides such as this one are useful, but they are merely designed to orientate you in the right direction. Ultimately, they are no substitute for your own responses which come from an in-depth knowledge and understanding of the text.

- Go through each chapter carefully, highlighting key passages from the text and noting down the quotes which strike you as relevant or significant.

- Sort out the quotes under headings: theme, characterisation. Memorise five or six general quotes which can be incorporated into your exam response.

- Charts are helpful in terms of clarifying your ideas. For example, against each character's name, you might list their positive and negative qualities, what motivates them, influences them, and so on. Remember, character is revealed by what individuals say, what they do, and what others say about them.

- Construct a timeline. This is particularly useful with a text like *The Great Gatsby* where the time scheme jumps back and forth.

- *Reflect* on the issues raised. To what extent did you identify with the characters? Are there any connections between the situations in which the characters find themselves and your own experiences? What, if anything, did the text teach you about human relationships, the human condition in general?

- Devise your own essay topics. Plan responses to these. While the creative question has been deleted from the exam, writing these responses are still a valuable revision tool in terms of enhancing your understanding of the text.

REFERENCES & READING

Text

Fitzgerald, F. Scott, *The Great Gatsby*, with Introduction and Notes by Tony Tanner, Twentieth Century Classics, Penguin, Harmondsworth, 2000.

Video

The Great Gatsby by F. Scott Fitzgerald, presented by Alan Dilnot and Richard Pannell, Video Classroom, Melbourne, 1985.

Websites

'F. Scott Fitzgerald Centenary', *University of South Carolina*, 2002, http://www.sc.edu/fitzgerald/

'Weblinks for English: The Great Gatsby', *Melbourne High School Library*, 2005, http://resources.mhs.vic.edu.au/class/english/textlink.htm#gatsby *Text discussion page on* The Great Gatsby *by Melbourne High School. This includes chat-lines, notes, essays and links to other Gatsby sites on the web.*

Other references

Berman, Ronald, *The Great Gatsby in Modern Times*, University of Illinois Press, Urbana, 1994.

Broccoli, Matthew J., *New Essays on the The Great Gatsby*, Cambridge University Press, New York, 1985.

Donaldson, Scott (ed.), *Critical Essays on The Great Gatsby*, G. K. Hall, Boston, Massachusetts, 1984.

Lockridge, Ernest H., *Twentieth Century Interpretations of The Great Gatsby: a collection of critical essays*, Prentice-Hall, Englewood Cliffs, N. J., 1968.

notes

1-12

CPSIA information can be obtained at www.ICGtesting.com
Printed in the USA
LVOW010627221111

255892LV00001B/7/P